Shargunam S
Mallika Pandeeswari R
Ravi R

Definitive Guide to Cloud Computing

Shargunam S
Mallika Pandeeswari R
Ravi R

Definitive Guide to Cloud Computing

Effective guidelines for Cloud Computing

Noor Publishing

Cover image: www.ingimage.com

Publisher:
Noor Publishing
is a trademark of
Dodo Books Indian Ocean Ltd., member of the OmniScriptum S.R.L Publishing group
str. A.Russo 15, of. 61, Chisinau-2068, Republic of Moldova Europe
Printed at: see last page
ISBN: 978-620-3-85790-0

DEFINITIVE GUIDE TO CLOUD COMPUTING

S. Shargunam, R.Mallika@pandeeswari, Dr. R. Ravi

TABLE OF CONTENTS

UNIT-1

CLOUD COMPUTING FUNDAMENTALS

1.1.MOTIVATION

Allow us to audit the situation of processing before the declaration and accessibility of distributed computing: The clients who are needing figuring are required to put away cash on processing assets like equipment, programming, systems administration, and capacity; this venture normally costs a mass money to the clients as they need to purchase these registering assets, keep these in their premises, and keep up and make it operational—every one of these assignments would add cost. Also, this is an especially obvious and immense consumption to the endeavours that require tremendous figuring force and assets, contrasted and traditional scholastics and people. Then again, it is simple and convenient to get the necessary figuring force and assets from some supplier (or provider) as and when it is required and pay just for that use. This would cost just a sensible venture or spending, contrasted with the immense speculation when purchasing the whole registering foundation. This wonder can be seen as capital consumption versus operational use. As one can undoubtedly survey the tremendous knot total needed for capital use (entire venture and upkeep for figuring foundation) and contrast it and the moderate or more modest protuberance total needed for the recruiting or getting the registering framework just to the tune of required time, and rest of the time liberated from that. Subsequently, cloud figuring is an instrument of bringing–recruiting or getting the administrations of the processing force or foundation to an authoritative or individual level to the degree required and paying just for the devoured administrations.

One can contrast the present circumstance and the utilization of power (its administrations) from its maker cum-wholesaler (in India, it is the state-/government-possessed power sheets that give power supply to all homes and associations) to houses or associations; here, we don't create power (similar with power creation related undertakings); rather, we use it just to tune up our necessities in our premises, for example, for our lighting and utilization of other electrical machines, and pay according to the power meter understanding worth.

In this way, distributed computing is required in getting the administrations of registering assets. Accordingly, one can say as a one-line answer to the requirement for cloud registering that it kills an enormous processing venture without trading off the utilization of figuring at the client level at an operational expense. Cloud registering is conservative and sets aside a ton of cash. A visually impaired advantage of this processing is that regardless of whether we lose our PC or because of some emergency our PC—and the work area framework—gets harmed, still our information what's more, records will remain safe and got as these are not in our neighbourhood machine (but rather distantly situated at the supplier's place—machine).

1.2.NEED FOR CLOUD COMPUTING

The primary explanations behind the need and utilization of distributed computing are accommodation and dependability. Previously, in the event that we needed to bring a record, we would need to save it to a Widespread Serial Bus (USB) streak drive, outer hard drive, or minimal circle (CD) also, carry that gadget to a better place. All things considered, saving a document to the cloud (e.g., utilization of cloud application Dropbox) guarantees that we will actually want to get to it with any PC that has an Internet association. The cloud likewise makes it much simpler to impart a record to companions, making it conceivable to work together ridiculous.

While utilizing the cloud, losing our information/document is substantially less likely. Notwithstanding, actually like anything on the web, there is consistently a danger that somebody may attempt to acquire admittance to our own information, and in this way, it is imperative to pick an entrance control with a solid secret word and focus on any security settings for the cloud administration that we are utilizing.

1.3.CLOUD COMPUTING DEFINITION

Cloud computing is a model for conveying data benefits that gives adaptable utilization of virtual workers, enormous versatility, and the board administrations. With the word reference definition far removed, we would now be able to continue to depicting distributed computing as far as its fundamental highlights and how it capacities close by other data advances. Distributed computing is a one of a kind blend of capacities which include:

- An enormously adaptable, powerful foundation
- Universal access
- Fine-grained use controls and valuing

- Standardized stages
- Management support administrations

1.3.1 NIST DEFINITION OF CLOUD COMPUTING

The formal definition of cloud computing comes from the National Institute of Standards and Technology (NIST): "Cloud computing is a model for enabling ubiquitous, convenient, on-demand network access to a shared pool of configurable computing resources (e.g., networks, servers, storage, applications, and services) that can be rapidly provisioned and released with minimal management effort or service provider interaction. It implies that the figuring asset or framework—be it worker equipment, capacity, organization, or application programming—all accessible from the cloud merchant or on the other hand supplier's website/premises, can be open preposterous from any distant area and by any nearby processing gadget. Furthermore, the utilization or openness is to cost uniquely to the degree of use to the clients dependent on their necessities and requests, otherwise called the pay-more only as costs arise or pay-according to utilize model. On the off chance that the need is more, more quantum figuring assets are made accessible (provisioning with flexibility) by the supplier. Insignificant administration exertion suggests that at the client's side, the support of registering frameworks is negligible as they should take a gander at these assignments just for their nearby processing gadgets utilized for getting to cloud-based assets, not for those registering assets oversaw at the supplier's side.

1.4.WHY USE CLOUD COMPUTING

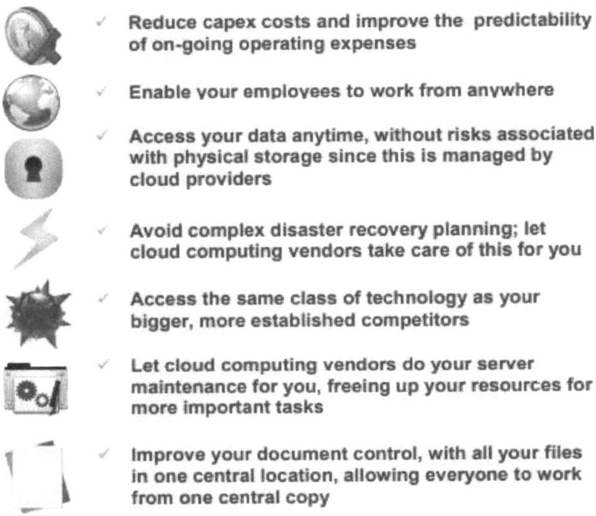

1.5.PRINCIPLES OF CLOUD COMPUTING

The 5-4-3 principles put forth by NIST describe (a) the five essential characteristic features that promote cloud computing, (b) the four deployment models that are used to narrate the cloud computing opportunities for customers while looking at architectural models, and (c) the three important and basic service offering models of cloud computing.

1.5.1 FIVE ESSENTIAL CHARACTERISTICS

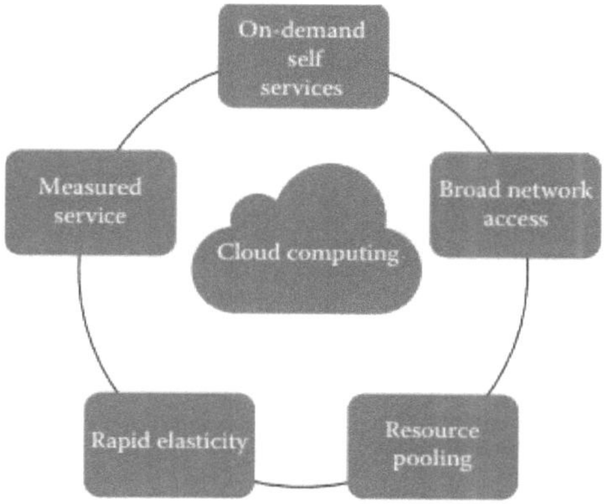

Figure 1.1 Characteristics of cloud computing

Cloud computing has five fundamental attributes, which are appeared in Figure 1.1. Per users can take note of the word fundamental, which implies that if any of these qualities is missing, at that point it isn't distributed computing:

1. On-demand self-services: A customer can singularly arrangement registering capacities, for example, worker time and organization stockpiling, as required naturally without requiring human cooperation with each specialist organizations.

2. Broad Network access: Capabilities are accessible ridiculous and gotten to through standard components that advance use by heterogeneous slight or thick customer stages (e.g., cell phones, PCs, furthermore, individual advanced collaborators [PDAs]).

3. Elastic resource pooling: The supplier's registering assets are pooled to serve different purchasers utilizing a multitenant model, with distinctive physical and virtual assets progressively appointed and reassigned by buyer interest. There is a feeling of area autonomy in that the client for the most part has no control or information over the specific area of the gave assets yet may have the option to determine the area at a more significant level of deliberation (e.g., nation, state, or server farm). Instances of assets incorporate capacity, handling, memory, and organization transfer speed.

4. Rapid Elasticity: Capabilities can be quickly and flexibly provisioned, sometimes naturally, to rapidly scale out and quickly delivered to rapidly scale in. To the customer, the abilities accessible for provisioning frequently have all the earmarks of being limitless and can be bought in any amount whenever.

5. Measured Service: Cloud frameworks consequently control and streamline asset use by utilizing a metering capacity at some degree of deliberation fitting to the kind of administration (e.g., capacity, preparing, transfer speed, and dynamic client accounts). Asset use can be checked, controlled, and announced giving straightforwardness to both the supplier and purchaser of the used assistance.

1.5.2 FOUR DEPLOYMENT MODEL

Organization models portray the ways with which the cloud administrations can be conveyed or made accessible to its clients, contingent upon the hierarchical structure and the provisioning area. One can comprehend it thusly as well: cloud (Internet)- based figuring assets—that is, the areas where information and administrations are obtained and provisioned to its clients— can take different structures. Four arrangement models are normally recognized, specifically, public, private, local area, and cross breed cloud administration utilization:

1. Private cloud: The cloud foundation is provisioned for selective use by a solitary association containing various customers (e.g., specialty units). It could be possessed, overseen, and worked by the association, an outsider, or a mix of them, and it might exist on or off premises.

2. Public cloud: The cloud framework is provisioned for open use by the overall population. It could be claimed, overseen, and worked by a business, scholarly, or government association, or a mix of them. It exists anywhere nearby of the cloud supplier.

3. Community cloud: The cloud foundation is shared by a few associations and supports a particular local area that has shared concerns (e.g., mission, security prerequisites, strategy, and consistence contemplations). It could be overseen by the associations or a third party and may exist on premise or off premise.

4. Hybrid cloud: The cloud foundation is a structure of two or more unmistakable cloud foundations (private, local area, or public) that stay exceptional substances yet are bound together by normalized or then again exclusive innovation that empowers information and application convey ability (e.g., cloud blasting for load adjusting between mists).

1.5.3 THREE SERVICE OFFERING MODEL

The three sorts of administrations with which the cloud-based registering assets are accessible to end clients are as per the following: Software as a Service (SaaS),

Stage as a Service (PaaS), and Infrastructure as a Service (IaaS). It is too known as the help stage framework (SPI) model of the cloud and is appeared in Figure 1.2. SaaS is a product conveyance model in which applications (programming, which is perhaps the main registering assets) are facilitated by a merchant or specialist organization and made accessible to clients over an organization, normally the Internet. PaaS is a worldview for conveying working frameworks and related administrations (e.g., PC supported programming [CASE] apparatuses, incorporated advancement conditions [IDEs] for creating programming arrangements) over the Internet without downloads or establishment. IaaS includes revaluating the gear used to help activities, including capacity, equipment, workers, and systems administration parts.

1. **Cloud SaaS:** The capacity gave to the buyer is to utilize the supplier's applications running on a cloud framework, including network, workers, working frameworks, stockpiling, and surprisingly singular application capacities, with the conceivable exemption of restricted client explicit application design settings. The applications are available from different customer gadgets through either a flimsy customer interface, like an internet browser (e.g., electronic email), or a program interface. The buyer doesn't oversee or control the fundamental cloud foundation. Average applications offered as an assistance incorporate client relationship the board (CRM), business insight investigation, and internet bookkeeping programming.

2. **Cloud PaaS:** The ability gave to the shopper is to convey onto the cloud framework shopper made or obtained applications made utilizing programming dialects, libraries, administrations, and devices upheld by the supplier. The purchaser doesn't oversee or control the fundamental cloud framework yet has authority over the sent applications and perhaps design settings for the application-facilitating climate. At the end of the day, it is a bundled also, prepared to-run advancement or working system. The PaaS seller gives the organizations, workers, and capacity and oversees the degrees of adaptability and upkeep. The customer regularly pays for administrations utilized. Instances of PaaS suppliers incorporate Google App Motor and Microsoft Azure Services.

3. **Cloud IaaS:** The ability gave to the customer is to arrangement handling, stockpiling, organizations, and other crucial registering assets on a compensation for each utilization premise where the person in question can send what's more, run self-assertive

programming, which can incorporate working frameworks also, applications. The shopper doesn't oversee or control the fundamental cloud foundation yet has command over the working frameworks, stockpiling, and conveyed applications and potentially restricted control of select systems administration segments (e.g., have firewalls). The specialist co-op possesses the gear and is liable for lodging, cooling activity, and support. Amazon Web Services (AWS) is a mainstream illustration of a huge IaaS supplier.

The significant distinction among PaaS and IaaS is the measure of control that clients have. Fundamentally, PaaS permits sellers to oversee everything, while IaaS requires greater administration from the client side. As a rule, associations that as of now have a product bundle or application for an explicit reason and need to introduce and run it in the cloud ought to select to utilize IaaS rather than PaaS.

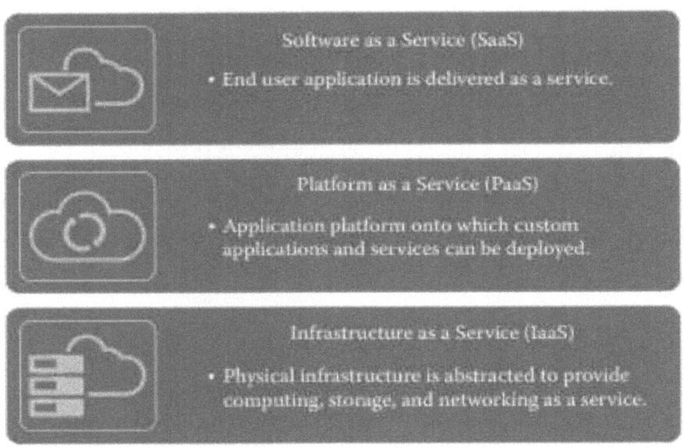

Figure 1.2 SPI—service offering model of the cloud

UNIT-2

CLOUD COMPUTING ARCHITECTURE AND MANAGEMENT

2.1. INTRODUCTION

Cloud computing is like different advancements such that it additionally has a few fundamental ideas that one ought to learn prior to knowing its center ideas. There are a few cycles and segments of distributed computing that should be examined. One of the subjects of such prime significance is design. Design is the various levelled perspective on portraying an innovation. This typically incorporates the parts over which the current innovation is fabricated and the segments that are reliant upon the innovation. Another subject that is identified with design is life structures. Life systems depicts the center construction of the cloud. When the design of the cloud is clear, the organization associations in the cloud and the insights concerning the cloud application should be known. This is significant as the cloud is a totally Internet-subordinate innovation. Also, cloud the board examines the significant administration issues and manners by which the current cloud situation is overseen. It depicts the manner in which an application and foundation in the cloud are overseen. The executives is significant due to the nature of administration (QoS) factors that are associated with the cloud. These QoS factors structure the reason for distributed computing. Every one of the administrations are given dependent on these QoS factors. Likewise, application movement to the cloud additionally assumes a vital part. Not everything applications can be straightforwardly sent to the cloud. An application should be appropriately relocated to the cloud to be viewed as a legitimate cloud application that will have every one of the properties of the cloud.

2.2. CLOUD ARCHITECTURE

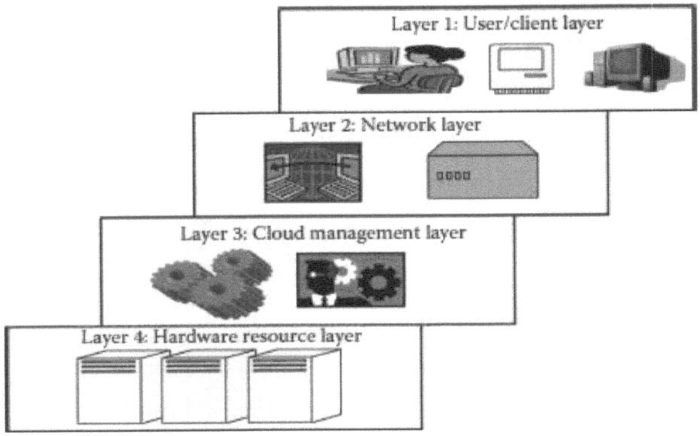

Figure 2.1 Cloud Architecture

2.2.1 User/Client Layer

This layer is the least layer in the cloud engineering. Every one of the clients or customer have a place with this layer. This is where the customer/client starts the association with the cloud. The customer can be any gadget like a slender customer, thick customer, or portable or any handheld gadget that would uphold fundamental functionalities to get to a web application. The meagre customer here alludes to a gadget that is totally subject to some other framework for its total usefulness. In basic terms, they have extremely low preparing capacity. Also, thick customers are general PCs that have sufficient handling ability. They have adequate capacity for autonomous work. Normally, a cloud application can be gotten too similarly as a web application. Yet, inside, the properties of cloud applications are fundamentally extraordinary. Along these lines, this layer comprises of customer gadgets.

2.2.2 Network Layer

This layer permits the clients to interface with the cloud. The entire cloud framework is reliant upon this association where the administrations are offered to the clients. This is basically the Internet on account of a public cloud. The public cloud as a rule exists in a particular area and the client would not have the foggiest idea about the area as it is unique. Furthermore, the public cloud can be gotten to everywhere on the world. On account of a private cloud, the availability might be given by a neighbourhood (LAN). Indeed, even for this situation, the cloud totally relies upon the organization that is utilized. Normally, while getting to people in general or private cloud, the clients require least data transfer capacity, which is here and there characterized by the cloud suppliers. This layer doesn't go under the domain of administration level arrangements (SLAs), that is, SLAs don't consider the Internet association between the client and cloud for nature of administration (QoS).

2.2.3 Cloud Management Layer

This layer comprises of virtual products that are utilized in dealing with the cloud. The virtual products can be a cloud working framework (OS), a product that goes about as an interface between the server farm (real assets) and the client, or an administration programming that permits overseeing assets. These virtual products for the most part permit asset the board (booking, provisioning, and so on), improvement (worker solidification, stockpiling responsibility union), and interior cloud administration. This layer goes under the domain of SLAs, that is, the activities occurring in this layer would influence the SLAs that are being chosen between the clients and the specialist organizations. Any postponement in preparing or any error in help provisioning may prompt a SLA infringement. According to rules, any SLA infringement would bring about a punishment to be given by the specialist organization. These SLAs are for both private and public mists popular specialist co-ops are Amazon Web Services (AWS) and Microsoft Azure for public cloud. Additionally, Open Stack and Eucalyptus permit private cloud creation, sending, and the board.

2.2.4 Hardware Resource Layer

Layer 4 comprises of arrangements for real equipment assets. Ordinarily, on account of a public cloud, a server farm is utilized in the back end. Likewise, in a private cloud, it very well may be a server farm, which is a colossal assortment of equipment assets interconnected to one another that is available in a particular area or a high arrangement framework. This layer goes under the domain of SLAs. This is the main layer that oversees the SLAs. This layer influences the SLAs most on account of server farms. At whatever point a client gets to the cloud, it ought to be accessible to the clients as fast as could really be expected and ought to be inside the time that is characterized by the SLAs. As referenced, if there is any error in provisioning the assets or application, the specialist organization needs to suffer the consequence. Thus, the server farm comprises of a rapid organization association and an exceptionally effective calculation to move the information from the server farm to the supervisor. There can be various server farms for a cloud, and comparably, various mists can share a server farm.

Hence, this is the design of a cloud. The layering is severe, and for any cloud application, this is followed. There can be a little free separation between layer 3 and layer 4 relying upon the manner in which the cloud is sent.

2.3 CLOUD ANATOMY

Cloud life systems can be essentially characterized as the design of the cloud. Cloud life structures can't be viewed as equivalent to cloud engineering. It may exclude any reliance on which or over which the innovation works, while design completely characterizes and depicts the innovation over which it is working. Engineering is a various levelled underlying perspective that characterizes the innovation just as the innovation over which it is reliant or/and the innovation that are subject to it. Hence, life structures can be considered as a piece of engineering. The essential construction of the cloud is depicted in Figure 2.2, which can be explained, and minute underlying subtleties can be given. Figure 2.2 portrays the most standard life structures that is the base for the cloud. It relies upon the individual to pick the profundity of portrayal of the cloud.

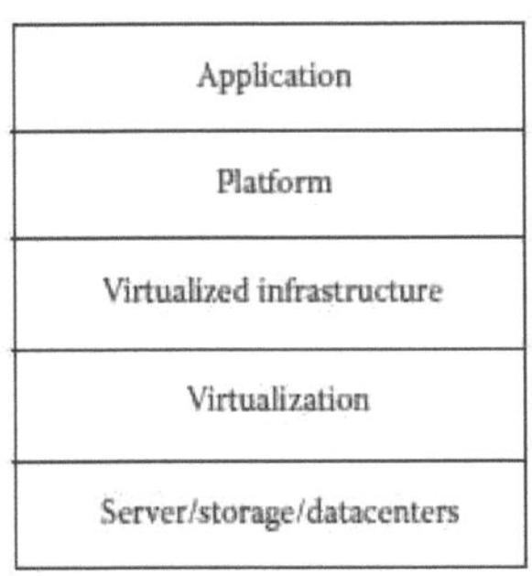

Figure 2.2 Cloud Structure

There are essentially five segments of the cloud:

1. Application: The upper layer is the application layer. In this layer, any applications are executed.

2. Stage: This part comprises of stages that are liable for the execution of the application. This stage is between the framework and the application.

3. Framework: The foundation comprises of assets over which different segments work. This gives computational ability to the client.

4. Virtualization: Virtualization is the way toward making consistent parts of assets over the current actual assets. The legitimate segments are disengaged and autonomous, which structure the framework.

5. Actual equipment: The actual equipment is given by worker and capacity units.

2.4 NETWORK CONEECTIVITY IN CLOUD COMPUTING

Cloud computing is a strategy of asset sharing where workers, stockpiling, and other figuring framework in various areas are associated by networks. In the cloud, when an application is submitted for its execution, penniless and appropriate assets are apportioned from this assortment of assets; as these assets are associated through the Internet, the clients get their necessary outcomes. For some, distributed computing applications, network execution will be the central point of contention to distributed computing execution. Since distributed computing has different organization choices, we currently consider the significant perspectives identified with the cloud arrangement models and their availability from the perspective of organization network.

2.4.1 PUBLIC CLOUD ACCESS NETWORKING

In this choice, the availability is frequently through the Internet, however some cloud suppliers might have the option to help virtual private organizations (VPNs) for clients. Getting to public cloud administrations will consistently make issues identified with security, which thus is identified with execution. One of the potential methodologies toward the help of safety is to advance network through scrambled passages, so the data might be sent by means of secure lines on the Internet. This system will be an overhead in the network, and utilizing it will absolutely build delay and may affect execution.

In the event that we need to lessen the deferral without bargaining security, we need to choose an appropriate steering strategy, for example, the one decreasing the postponement by limiting travel bounces eventually to-end network between the cloud supplier and cloud buyer. Since the start to finish network support is by means of the Internet, which is a mind boggling alliance of interconnected suppliers (known as Internet specialist co-ops [ISPs]), one needs to take a gander at the alternatives of choosing the way.

2.4.2 PRIVATE CLOUD ACCESS NETWORKING

In the private cloud sending model, since the cloud is essential for a hierarchical organization, the innovation and approaches are nearby to the in-house network structure. This may incorporate an Internet VPN or VPN administration from an organization administrator. On the off chance that the application access was appropriately finished with a hierarchical organization—network in a precloud design—change to private distributed computing won't influence the entrance execution.

2.4.3 INTRACLOUD NETWORKING

Another organization availability thought in distributed computing is intracloud organizing for public cloud administrations. Here, the assets of the cloud supplier and subsequently the cloud administration to the client depend on the assets that are topographically separated from one another yet associated through the Internet. Public distributed computing networks are interior to the specialist organization and in this manner not noticeable to the client/client; be that as it may, the security parts of availability and the entrance instruments of the assets are significant. Another issue to search for is the QoS in the associated assets around the world. A large portion of the presentation issues and infringement from these are tended to in the SLAs economically.

2.4.4 PRIVATE INTRACLOUD NETWORKING

The most convoluted issue for systems administration and availability in distributed computing is private intracloud organizing. What makes this specific issue so perplexing is that it relies upon how much intracloud network is related with the applications being executed in this climate? Private Intracloud organizing is normally upheld over network between the significant server farm destinations possessed by the organization. At the very least, all distributed computing executions will depend on intracloud systems administration to interface clients with the asset to which their application was alloted. When the asset linkage is made, the degree to which intracloud organizing is utilized relies upon whether the application is componentized dependent on help situated design (SOA) or not, among various frameworks. On the off chance that the standard of SOA is followed, traffic may move between parts of the application, just as between the application and the client. The exhibition of those associations will at that point sway distributed computing execution generally. Here as well, the effect of distributed computing execution is the distinctions that exist between the current application and the organization associations with the application.

There are motivations to consider the organizations and availability in distributed computing with more up to date approaches as globalization and changing organization prerequisites, particularly those identified with expanded Internet use, are requesting greater adaptability in the organization models of the present endeavours. How are these identified with us? The appropriate responses are talked about later.

2.4.5 NEW FACETS IN PRIVATE NETWORK

Regular private organizations have been architected for on-premise applications and most extreme Internet security. Commonly, applications, for example, email, document sharing, and venture asset arranging (ERP) frameworks are conveyed to on-premise-based workers at each corporate server farm. Progressively today, programming merchants are offering Software as a Service (SaaS) as an option for their product backing to the corporate workplaces, which acquires more difficulties the entrance and utilization components of programming from server farm workers and in the availability of organization structures. The customary organization engineering for these worldwide ventures was not intended to streamline execution for cloud applications, since numerous applications including strategic applications are progressing (moving) from on-premise based to cloud based, wherein the organization accessibility becomes as crucial as power: the business can't work on the off chance that it can't get to applications, for example, ERP and email.

2.4.6 PATH FOR ITERNAL TRAFFIC

The customary Internet traffic through a restricted arrangement of Internet entryways presents execution and accessibility issues for end clients who are utilizing cloud-based applications. It tends to be improved if an all the more generally dispersed Internet entryway foundation and network are being upheld for getting to applications, as they will give lower-inactivity admittance to their cloud applications. As the volume of traffic to cloud applications develops, the level of the inheritance organization's ability as far as traffic to local doors increments. Applications, for example, video conferencing would hoard more transmission capacity while strategic applications, for example, ERP will devour less transfer speed, and subsequently, one needs to design a right availability and way among suppliers and purchasers.

CHAPTER 3

VIRTUALIZATION

3.1 INTRODUCTION

Virtualization is the "making of a virtual (instead of genuine) rendition of something, like a worker, a work area, a capacity gadget, a working framework or organization assets". As such, Virtualization is a method, which permits to share a solitary actual example of an asset or an application among various clients and associations. It does by doling out a coherent name to an actual stockpiling and giving a pointer to that actual asset when requested.

3.1.1 WHAT IS THE CONCEPT BEHIND THE VIRTUALIZATION?

Formation of a virtual machine over existing working framework and equipment is known as Hardware Virtualization. A Virtual machine gives a climate that is sensibly isolated from the fundamental equipment. The machine on which the virtual machine will make is known as Host Machine and that virtual machine is alluded as a Guest Machine.
Few methodologies or approaches to virtualize cloud workers.

These are:

1. Network Approach: where the handling responsibilities are conveyed among various actual workers, and their outcomes are then gathered as one.

2. Operating system - Level Virtualization: Here, numerous occasions of an application can run in a confined structure on a solitary OS

3. Hypervisor-based Virtualization: which is as of now the most broadly utilized method

With hypervisor's virtualization, there are different sub-ways to deal with satisfy the objective of running numerous applications and different burdens on a solitary actual host. A method is utilized to permit virtual machines to move starting with one host then onto the next without closing down. This method is named as "Live Migration". Another strategy is utilized to effectively stack balance among numerous hosts to use those accessible assets in a virtual machine proficiently. The idea is named as Distributed Resource Scheduling or Dynamic Resource Scheduling.

3.1.2 HOW VIRTUALIZATION WORKS IN CLOUD COMPUTING?

Virtualization assumes a huge part in cloud innovation and its functioning instrument. Normally, what occurs in the cloud - the clients not just offer the information that are situated in the cloud-like application yet additionally share their foundations with the assistance of virtualization. Virtualization is utilized principally to furnish applications with standard forms for cloud clients. With the arrival of the most recent rendition of an application, the suppliers can proficiently give that application to the cloud and its clients, and it is conceivable utilizing virtualization as it were. By utilizing this virtualization idea, all workers and programming other cloud suppliers require those are kept up by an outsider, and the cloud supplier pays them on a month to month or yearly premise.

In actuality, the greater part of the present hypervisors utilize a mix of various kinds of equipment virtualization. Mostly virtualization implies running numerous frameworks on a solitary machine yet sharing all assets (equipment) and it assists with sharing IT assets to get benefits in the business field.

3.1.3 DIFFERENCE BETWEEN VIRTUALIZATION AND CLOUD?

- Essentially there is a gap between these two terms, though cloud technology requires the concept of virtualization. Virtualization is a technology - it can also be treated as software that can manipulate hardware. At the same time, cloud computing is a service that is the result of manipulation.

- Virtualization is the foundation element of cloud computing, whereas Cloud technology is the delivery of shared resources as a service-on-demand via the internet. Cloud is essentially made-up of the concept of virtualization.

3.1.4 BENEFITS OF VIRTUALIZATION

- More adaptable and productive allotment of assets.
- Enhance advancement efficiency.
- It brings down the expense of IT framework.
- Remote access and quick versatility.
- High accessibility and calamity recuperation.
- Pay scrutinize of the IT framework on request.
- Enables running various working frameworks.

3.1.5 ADVANTAGE AND DISADVANTAGE OF VIRTUALIZATION

There are numerous advantages of Virtualization, similar to it enhances equipment asset usage, saves energy and expenses and makes it conceivable to run different applications and different working frameworks on a similar SERVER simultaneously. It builds the use, effectiveness, and adaptability of existing PC equipment.

1. Gives the capacity to oversee assets successfully.
2. Builds proficiency of IT tasks.
3. Accommodates simpler reinforcement and calamity recuperation.
4. Builds cost investment funds with decreased equipment consumption.
5. Inconveniences of virtualization are practically irrelevant when contrasted with the different benefits it offers.
6. Programming permitting costs.
7. The need to prepare IT, staff, in virtualization.

3.1.6 FEATURES OF VIRTUALIZATION:

- Parceling: Multiple virtual workers can run on an actual worker simultaneously.
- Epitome of information: All information on the virtual worker, including boot circles, is epitomized in a record design.
- Disconnection: The Virtual worker running on the actual worker is securely isolated and don't influence one another.

- Equipment Independence: When the virtual worker runs, it can relocate to an alternate equipment stage.

3.2 TYPES OF VIRTUALIZATION

Here are six methodologies to look at when talking about virtualization techniques in cloud computing:

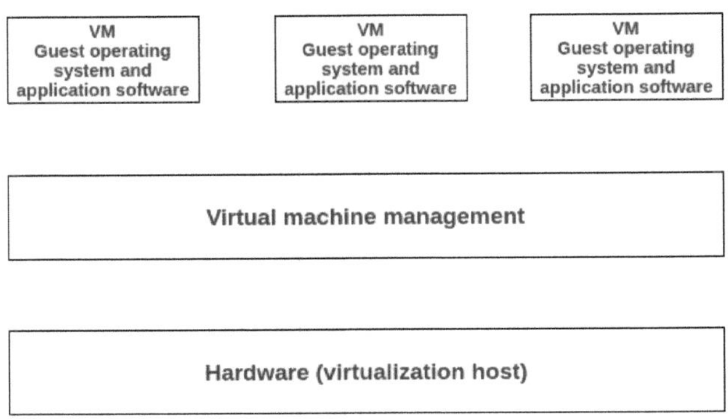

Figure 3.2.1 Hardware virtualization

3.2. 1 HARDWARE VIRTUALIZATION

It is the abstraction of computing resources from the software that uses cloud resources. It involves embedding virtual machine software into the server's hardware components. That software is called the hypervisor. The hypervisor manages the shared physical hardware resources between the guest OS & the host OS. The abstracted hardware is represented as actual hardware. Virtualization means abstraction & hardware virtualization is achieved by abstracting the physical hardware part using Virtual Machine Monitor (VMM) or hypervisor. Hypervisors rely on command set extensions in the processors to accelerate common virtualization activities for boosting the performance. The term hardware virtualization is used when VMM or virtual machine software or any hypervisor gets directly installed on the hardware system. The primary task of the hypervisor is to process monitoring, memory & hardware controlling. After hardware virtualization is done, different operating systems can be installed, and various applications can run on it. Hardware virtualization, when done for server platforms, is also called server virtualization.

3.2.1.1 ADVANTAGE OF HARDWARE VIRTUALIZATION

The advantages of equipment virtualization decline the general expense of cloud clients and increment adaptability. The benefits are:

- Lower Cost: Because of worker union, the expense diminishes; presently, numerous OS can exist together in a solitary equipment. This limits the amount of rack space, diminishes the quantity of workers, and ultimately drops the force utilization.

- Proficient asset usage: Physical assets can be divided between virtual machines. Another virtual machine can utilize the unused assets designated by one virtual machine if there should arise an occurrence of any need.

- Increment IT adaptability: The fast improvement of equipment assets became conceivable utilizing virtualization, and the assets can be overseen reliably moreover.

- Progressed Hardware Virtualization highlights: With the headway of present day hypervisors, exceptionally complex tasks augment the deliberation of equipment and guarantee most extreme uptime. This method assists with relocating a progressing virtual machine starting with one host then onto the next have progressively.

3.2.1.2 TYPES OF HARDWARE VIRTUALIZATION

Hardware virtualization is of three kinds. These are:

- Full Virtualization: Here, the equipment engineering is totally reproduced. Visitor programming needn't bother with any adjustment to run any applications.

- Emulation virtualization: Here, the virtual machine re-enacts the equipment and is free. Besides, the visitor OS doesn't need any adjustment.

- Para-Virtualization: Here, the equipment isn't reproduced; all things considered, the visitor programming runs its segregated framework.

3.2.2 SOFTWARE VIRTUALIZATION

Software Virtualization includes the making of an activity of different virtual conditions on the host machine. It makes a PC framework complete with equipment that lets the visitor working framework to run. For instance, it allows you to run Android OS on a host machine locally utilizing a Microsoft Windows OS, using a similar equipment as the host machine does.

3.2.2.1 TYPES OF SOFTWARE VIRTUALIZATION

- Operating system Virtualization – facilitating numerous OS on the local OS.
- Application Virtualization – facilitating singular applications in a virtual climate separate from the local OS.
- Administration Virtualization – facilitating explicit cycles and administrations identified with a specific application.

3.2.2.2 BENEFITS OF SOFTWARE VIRTUALIZATION

Here, is the list of Software Virtualization Advantages in Cloud Computing:

1. **Testing**

It is easier to test the new operating system and software on VMs as it does not require any additional hardware and the testing can do within the same software. After the testing, the VM can move or delete for the further testing.

2. Utilization

In software virtualization, there is higher efficiency in resource utilization if it tunes correctly. The VM can modify as per the requirement such as the user can modify ram, drive space, etc. It requires very less amount of hardware as compared to the equivalent number of physical machines.

3. Efficient

It is efficient in a way such that it can run 12 virtual machines and eliminates the use of 12 physical boxes. This is the power cost as well as the cost of maintaining the server.

4. Less Downtime

The software is upgrading and the upgrade in the VMs can do when the VM is working. VM can modify when it is working or it is not working which means that the downtime of it is very less.

5. Flexible

It provides flexibility to the user so that the user can modify the software as per their demand. The modification can do within minutes and can adjust easily when the workload changes.

6. Secure

It can protect with many Hantaviruses. Moreover, there are several firewalls which prevent hacking and virus. The data in the software virtualization is safe as it stores in several different places so if the disaster takes place the data can retrieve easily.

3.2.2.3 HOW SOFTWARE VIRTUALIZATION IN CLOUD COMPUTING WORKS?

I. Reinforcement

With the assistance of programming virtualization, the whole working framework or worker establishment can be supported up. This additionally benefits in a manner that if the new worker hack simply re-establishing the past variant will permit running the worker.

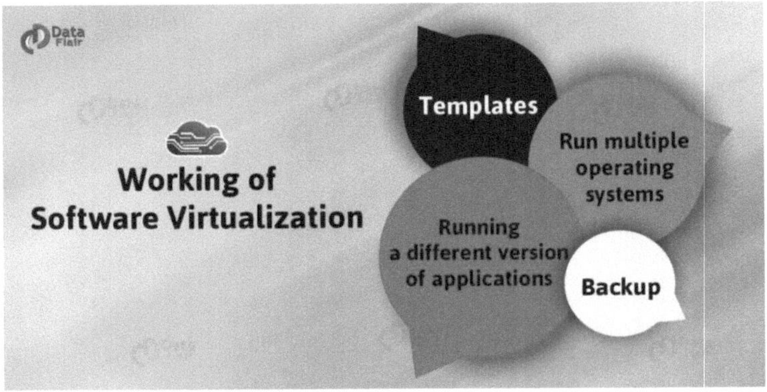

Figure: 3.2.2.3 Working of Software Virtualization

ii. Run numerous working frameworks

The distinctive working framework can use in a solitary PC with the parcel in the hard drive. The lone thing to remember is to keep a depiction of everything. On the off chance that the information suffocates, it can recover from some other spot.

iii. Running an alternate rendition of uses

With the assistance of programming virtualization new just as the old working framework can utilize. So a program, in the event that it isn't chipping away at a specific working framework, we can check it on another.

iv. Formats

After the setup of VM according to the interest, it can change over into a format and this layout can use to make various duplicates of the first one.

3.2.3 OPERATING SYSTEM VIRTUALIZATION

As in cloud innovation, virtualization assumes a significant part to make things simple and effectively done, virtualization likewise should be done at the OS level moreover. With the procedure of virtualized OS, nothing is needed to be pre-introduced or forever stacked on the neighbourhood stockpiling gadget. Everything runs from network utilizing a virtual; re-enactment and that virtual plate is a circle picture (record) that distantly put away on a worker for example Capacity Area Network (SAN) or Non-Volatile Attached Storage (NAS).

3.2.3.1 DEFINING OPERATING SYSTEM VIRTUALIZATION

It is likewise called OS-level virtualization is a kind of virtualization innovation which work on OS layer. Here the part of an OS permits more than one disengaged client space examples to exist. Such occurrences are called compartments/programming holders or virtualization motors. At the end of the day, OS portion will run a solitary working framework and give that working framework's usefulness to duplicate on every one of the secluded parcels.

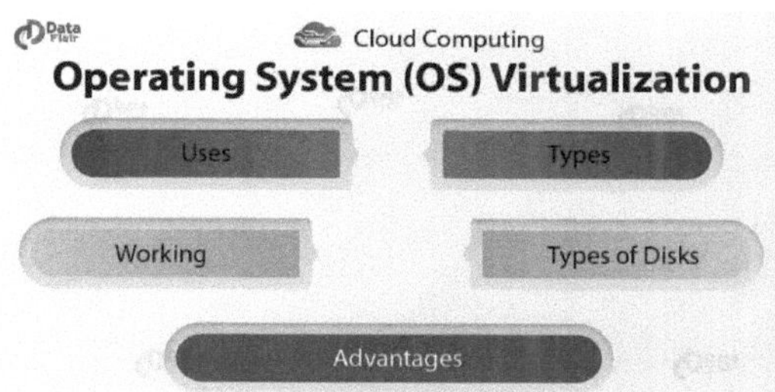

Figure 3.2.3.1: Working of OS Virtualization

3.2.3.2 USES OF OS VIRTUALIZATION

1. Utilized for virtual facilitating climate.

2. Utilized for safely portion of limited equipment assets among countless doubting clients.

3. Framework manager utilizes it to incorporate worker equipment by moving administrations on discrete hosts.

4. To ad libbed security by isolating a few applications to a few holders.

5. These types of virtualization don't expect equipment to work effectively.

3.2.3.3 STEPS FOR OS VIRTUALIZATION WORKS

The steps for how these virtualization works are listed below:

1. Connect to OS Virtualization Server
2. Connect to virtual disk
3. Then connect this virtual disk to the client
4. OS is streamed to the client
5. If further additional streaming is required, it is done.

3.2.3.4 TYPES OF OS VIRTUALIZATION

- Linux OS Virtualization
- Windows OS virtualizations

I. Linux Operating System virtualization

VMware Workstation programming is utilized to virtualize Linux frameworks. Moreover, to introduce any product by the methods for virtualization the client will require VMware programming to introduce first.

ii. Windows Operating System virtualizations

This kind of virtualization is likewise like the above to introduce any product there is a need to introduce VMware programming right off the bat.

3.2.3.5 KINDS OF DISKS IN OS VIRTUALIZATION

There are two sorts of virtual plate present in working framework virtualization with the goal that the customer can associate through the organization to the virtual circle.

I. Private Disk

The private circle uses by a solitary customer or single association. In this plate, the organization can store the data dependent on the capacity doled out.

ii. Shared Disk

Shared plate utilizes by different customers simultaneously. The progressions done by the customers are material independently and will not influence the settings of another customer hear that stores get cleaned when the framework is restarted. It will set to default after the framework gets a restart.

3.2.3.6 ADVANTAGE OF OS VIRTUALIZATION

1. Operating system virtualization normally forces practically zero overhead.

2. Operating system Virtualization is prepared to do live movement

3. It can likewise utilize dynamic burden adjusting of holders among hubs and a group.

The record level duplicate on-compose (CoW) system is conceivable on OS virtualization which makes simpler to back up documents, more space-effective and less complex to reserve than the square level duplicate on-compose plans.

3.2.3.7 FACTS ABOUT OS VIRTUALIZATION

- Working framework virtualization permits security and finds last IT equipment assets among an enormous number of commonly doubting clients.

- Besides, the framework executive uses it for combining worker equipment. This is finished by moving administrations on the different host in two holders which are on the worker.

- In working framework virtualization, the OS may conceal the assets with the goal that when the PC program peruses it they don't show up in the list results. Here it is additionally conceivable to run the program inside the compartments to which just pieces of these assets are distributed.

- A few compartments can present on each working arrangement of which a subset of the asset of the PC has been assigned.

- These holders contain various PC programs, this program can even communicate with one another. The patches and updates to the basic working framework are finished inside the length of time. In addition, they no affect the accessibility of utilization administrations.

- Along these lines, this was tied in with Operating System Virtualizations instructional exercise. Expectation you loved our clarification.

3.2.4 SERVER VIRTUALIZATION

It is the division of actual worker into a few virtual workers and this division is chiefly done to ad lib the utility of worker asset. In other word it is the veiling of assets that are situated in worker which incorporates the number and personality of processors, actual workers and the working framework. This division of one actual worker into numerous segregated virtual workers is finished by worker chairman utilizing programming. The virtual climate is once in a while called the virtual private-workers.

In this interaction, the worker assets are kept stowed away from the client. This parcelling of actual worker into a few virtual conditions; bring about the devotion of one worker to play out a solitary application or errand.

3.2.4.1 USAGE OF SERVER VIRTUALIZATION

This technique is mainly used in web-servers which reduces the cost of web-hosting services. Instead of having separate system for each web-server, multiple virtual servers can run on the same system/computer.

The primary uses of server virtualization are:

- To centralize the server administration
- Improve the availability of server
- Helps in disaster recovery

- Ease in development & testing
- Make efficient use of server resources.
- Approaches of Server Virtualization:

For Server Virtualization, there are three famous methodologies.

These are:

- Virtual Machine model
- Para-virtual Machine model

Working System (OS) layer Virtualization

Worker virtualization can be seen as a piece of in general virtualization pattern in the IT organizations that incorporate organization virtualization, stockpiling virtualization and the board of responsibility. This pattern acquires improvement programmed figuring. Worker virtualization can likewise used to dispose of worker spread (Server spread is a circumstance where numerous under-used workers use more space or burn-through a greater number of assets than can be legitimized by their responsibility) and utilizations worker assets productively.

- Virtual Machine model: depend on have visitor worldview, where every visitor runs on a virtual reproduction of equipment layer. This procedure of virtualization give visitor OS to run without adjustment. Anyway it requires genuine registering assets from the host and for this a hypervisor or VM is needed to facilitate directions to CPU.

- Para-Virtual Machine model: is likewise founded on have visitor worldview and utilizes virtual machine screen as well. In this model the VMM adjusts the visitor working framework's code which is called 'porting'. Like that of virtual machine, correspondingly the Para-virtual machine is likewise fit for executing various working frameworks. The Para-virtual model is utilized by both Xen and UML.

- Working System Layer Virtualization: Virtualization at OS level capacities in an alternate manner and did not depend on have visitor worldview. In this model the host runs a solitary working framework portion as its fundamental/center and moves its usefulness

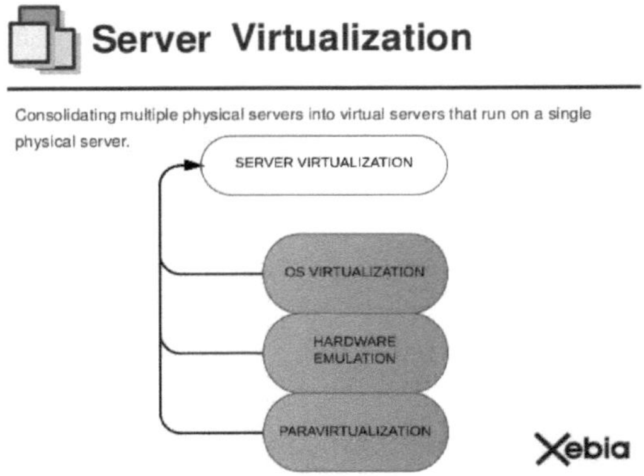

Fig 3.2.4.1 working of Server virtualization

to every one of the visitors. The visitor should utilize a similar working framework as the host. This dispersed nature of design killed framework calls among layers and thus diminishes overhead of CPU use. It is additionally an unquestionable requirement that each parcel remains stringently disconnected from its neighbors in light of the fact that any disappointment or security penetrate of one segment will not have the option to influence different parts.

3.2.4.2 ADVANTAGE OF SERVER VIRTUALIZATION

- Cost Reduction: Server virtualization lessens cost on the grounds that less equipment is required.

- Free Restart: Each worker can be rebooted autonomously and that reboot will not influence the working of other virtual workers.

3.2.5 MEMORY VIRTUALIZATION

Actual memory across various workers is totaled into a solitary virtualized memory pool. It gives the advantage of an augmented adjoining working memory. You may as of now be comfortable with this, as some OS, for example, Microsoft Windows OS permits a part of your stockpiling circle to fill in as an expansion of your RAM.

Types of Memory Virtualization:

- Application-level control – Applications access the memory pool straightforwardly
- Working framework level control – Access to the memory pool is given through a working framework.

3.2.6 DATA VIRTUALIZATION

This is the sort of virtualization wherein the information is gathered from different sources and dealt with that at a solitary spot without find out about the specialized data like how information is gathered, put away and designed then masterminded that information coherently so its virtual view can be gotten to by its intrigued individuals and partners, and clients through the different cloud benefits distantly. Numerous large goliath organizations are offering their types of assistance like Oracle, IBM, At scale, Cdata and so on

- It tends to be accustomed to performing different sort of errands, for example,
- Information incorporation
- Business-incorporation
- Administration arranged design information administrations
- Looking through authoritative information

3.2.6.1 ADVANTAGE OF DATA VIRTUALIZATION

There are the following advantages of data virtualization -

- It allows users to access the data without worrying about where it resides on the memory.
- It offers better customer satisfaction, retention, and revenue growth.
- It provides various security mechanism that allows users to safely store their personal and professional information.
- It reduces costs by removing data replication.
- It provides a user-friendly interface to develop customized views.
- It provides various simple and fast deployment resources.
- It increases business user efficiency by providing data in real-time.
- It is used to perform tasks such as data integration, business integration, Service-Oriented Architecture (SOA) data services, and enterprise search.

3.2.7 APPLICATION VIRTUALIZATION

In this kind of virtualization we use programming to make our application as a solitary executable record that can be run anyplace, this product will be isolated from our OS and we will run it in a sandbox. Application virtualization can additionally be partitioned into two classifications they are:

- Far off: In this kind of utilization virtualization, the customer will utilize a presentation convention that is far off to impart to the customer machine. One of the benefits of this sort of virtualization is that, since it is being utilized generally it is simple for setting up shows for different applications.

- Streaming: The excellence of this sort of use virtualization is that we will actually want to have a duplicate of the application on our worker and we can have them run equal in the nearby frameworks of customer, so on account of this overhauling, the application turns out to be a lot simpler as the customer will consistently highlight the most recent form.
- A couple of instances of utilization virtualization are Xenapp, VM Thinapp, and Zenworks.
-

3.2.8 STORAGE VIRTUALIZATION

Storage virtualization fundamentally consolidates/pools the capacity that is accessible in different gadgets and keeps it as single stockpiling. Distinguishing proof of the accessible stockpiling is finished by utilizing the product and totals them to utilize it in a virtual framework/climate. The product quite screens the different I/O demands from any virtual/actual framework and it blocks them and sends it to the suitable area where the joined stockpiles are kept up in a virtual climate. This procedure of capacity virtualization really helps the head for any recuperation or reinforcement or chronicled of information in a successful and productive way by taking nearly less time than the standard thing. A portion of the upsides of this sort of virtualization are:

- Our information doesn't get traded off effectively regardless of whether the host comes up short as we store our information in an alternate and advantageous spot.
- It is simple for us to secure, give and utilize our information as we execute some degree of reflection in our capacity.
- Extra capacities like recuperation, duplication, replication, and so on should be possible easily

3.3 HYPERVISIOR

A hypervisor is a type of virtualization programming utilized in Cloud facilitating to partition and apportion the assets on different bits of equipment. The program which gives dividing, disengagement or reflection is called virtualization hypervisor. The hypervisor is an equipment virtualization strategy that permits numerous visitor working frameworks (OS) to run on a solitary host framework simultaneously. A hypervisor is once in a while additionally called a virtual machine manager (VMM).

3.3.1 SORTS OF HYPERVISOR

TYPE-1 Hypervisor:

The hypervisor runs straightforwardly on the fundamental host framework. It is otherwise called "Local Hypervisor" or "Uncovered metal hypervisor". It doesn't need any base worker working framework. It has direct admittance to equipment assets. Instances of Type 1 hypervisors incorporate VMware ESXi, Citrix XenServer and Microsoft Hyper-V hypervisor.

Pros and Cons of Type-1 Hypervisor:

- Pros: Such sort of hypervisors are effective in light of the fact that they have direct admittance to the actual equipment resources(like Cpu, Memory, Network, Physical capacity). This causes the strengthening the security in light of the fact that there isn't anything any sort of the outsider asset so assailant couldn't bargain with anything.
- Cons : One issue with Type-1 hypervisor is that they normally need a devoted separate machine to play out its activity and to teach distinctive VMs and control the host equipment assets.

TYPE-2 Hypervisor:

A Host working framework runs on the basic host framework. It is otherwise called 'Facilitated Hypervisor". Such sort of hypervisors doesn't run straight preposterous equipment rather they run as an application in a Host system(physical machine). Essentially, programming introduced on a working framework. Hypervisor requests that the working framework settle on equipment decisions. Illustration of Type 2 hypervisor incorporates VMware Player or Parallels Desktop. Facilitated hypervisors are frequently found on endpoints like PCs. The sort 2 hypervisor is are helpful for engineers, security analyst (for checking malware, or malignant source code and recently created applications).

Pros and Cons of Type-2 Hypervisor:

- Pros: Such sort of hypervisors permits speedy and simple admittance to a visitor Operating System close by the host machine running. These hypervisors ordinarily accompany extra helpful highlights for visitor machine. Such instruments upgrade the coordination between the host machine and visitor machine.
- Cons: Here there is no immediate admittance to the actual equipment assets so the productivity of these hypervisors slacks in execution when contrasted with the kind 1 hypervisors, and potential security hazards are likewise there an assailant can bargain the security shortcoming if there is admittance to the host working framework so he can likewise get to the visitor working framework.

3.3.2 CHOOSING RIGHT HYPERVISIOR

Type 1 hypervisors offer much preferred execution over Type 2 ones on the grounds that there's no center layer, settling on them the consistent decision for crucial applications and responsibilities. However, this shouldn't imply that that facilitated hypervisors don't have their place – they're a lot easier to set up, so they're a decent wagered if, say, you need to send a test climate rapidly. Perhaps the most ideal approaches to figure out which hypervisor addresses your issues is to think about their exhibition measurements. These incorporate CPU overhead, measure of most extreme host and visitor memory, and backing for virtual processors. The accompanying variables ought to be inspected prior to picking an appropriate hypervisor:

1. Comprehend your requirements: The organization and its applications are the justification the server farm (and your work). Other than your organization's requirements, you (and your associates in IT) likewise have your own necessities. Needs for a virtualization hypervisor are:

a. Flexible

b. Adaptability

c. Ease of use

d. Accessibility

e. Dependability

f. Effectiveness

g. Solid help

2. The expense of a hypervisor: For some purchasers, the hardest piece of picking a hypervisor is finding some kind of harmony among cost and usefulness. While various section level arrangements are free, or basically free, the costs at the furthest edge of the market can be faltering. Permitting systems additionally shift, so it's imperative to know about precisely the thing you're getting for your cash.

3. Virtual machine execution: Virtual frameworks should meet or surpass the exhibition of their actual partners, in any event corresponding to the applications inside every worker. All that past gathering this benchmark is benefit.

4. Biological system: It's enticing to disregard the job of a hypervisor's environment – that is, the accessibility of documentation, support, preparing, outsider engineers and consultancies, etc – in deciding if an answer is savvy in the long haul.

5. Test for yourself: You can acquire essential experience from your current work area or PC. You can run both VMware vSphere and Microsoft Hyper-V in either VMware Workstation or VMware Fusion to make a decent virtual learning and testing climate.

Advantage of Hypervisor:

Despite the fact that virtual machines work on a similar actual equipment, they are isolated from one another. This likewise portrays that on the off chance that one virtual machine goes through an accident, blunder, or a malware assault, it doesn't influence the other virtual machines.

Another advantage is that virtual machines are exceptionally versatile as they don't rely upon the hidden equipment. Since they are not connected to actual equipment, exchanging between nearby or far off virtualized workers gets much simpler when contrasted with conventional applications.

3.3.3 HYPERVISOR REFERENCE MODEL

There are 3 fundamental modules organizes to imitate the basic equipment:

DISPATCHER:

- The dispatcher carries on like the section point of the screen and reroutes the directions of the virtual machine occasion to one of the other two modules.

ALLOCATOR:

- The allocator is liable for choosing the framework assets to be given to the virtual machine instance.It implies at whatever point virtual machine attempts to execute a guidance that outcomes in changing the machine assets related with the virtual machine, the allocator is summoned by the dispatcher.

Translator:

- The translator module comprises of mediator routines.These are executed, at whatever point virtual machine executes a priviliged guidance.

Another helpful component it offers is inherent administration, which implies you don't have to sign in to and work through the hypervisor. For security purposes, the instrument additionally incorporates worked in observing and alarms, to help ensure your hypervisor isn't settled.

CHAPTER 4

WEB 2.0

4.1 INTODUCTION

Web 2.0 alludes to overall site which feature client created substance, ease of use and interoperability for end clients. Web 2.0 is likewise called participative social web. It doesn't allude to an adjustment to any specialized particular, however to change in the manner in which Web pages are planned and utilized. The progress is advantageous yet it doesn't appear to be that when the progressions are happened. A cooperation and coordinated effort with one another is permitted by Web 2.0 in an online media exchange as maker of client produced content in a virtual local area. Web 1.0 is improved form of Web 2.0.

The internet browser advancements are utilized in Web 2.0 turn of events and it incorporates AJAX and JavaScript structures. As of late, AJAX and JavaScript systems have become an extremely well known methods for making web 2.0 locales.

4.1.1 FIVE SIGNIFICANT HIGHLIGHTS OF WEB 2.0

- Free arranging of data, grants clients to recover and group the data by and large.
- Dynamic substance that is responsive to customer input. Information streams between page owner and site customers by strategies for appraisal.
- Created APIs to permit self-utilization, for example, by a product application.
- Web access prompts concern extraordinary, from the customary Internet client base to a more extensive assortment of clients.

4.1.2 UTILIZATION OF WEB 2.0

The social Web contains various online devices and stages where individuals share their points of view, sentiments, musings and encounters. Web 2.0 applications will in general interface considerably more with the end client. Taking everything into account, the end customer isn't only a customer of the application yet moreover a part by these 8 gadgets referred to underneath:

- Writing for a blog

- Labeling
- Curating with RSS
- Social bookmarking
- Long range informal communication
- Web-based media
- Web content democratic

4.1.3 PROS AND CONS OF WEB 2.0

Pros Web 2.0

- Web-based Media Marketing and Search Engine Optimization.
- Equivalent opportunity to all to post their perspectives and remarks.
- Increment the circles and contacts through long range informal communication.
- Most recent updates and substance can be gotten on the off chance that you are a RSS peruser.
- Online advancement of organizations, items, and administrations.
- Drawing in clients. Clients can compose their perspectives about items and administrations.

Cons web 2.0

- Data over-burden. An excess of data is day by day posted by numerous individuals with various contemplations. This makes disarray for the perusers and the nature of the substance isn't dependable.
- Opportunity to post perspectives and remarks gives great freedoms to contenders and opponents to post negative remarks about different organizations.
- Too many phony ids and spammers.
- Phonies and programmers perpetrate wrongdoings.

4.2 WEB-BASED MEDIA MARKETING

Web-based MEDIA MARKETING is one of the greatest and most critical consequences of Web 2.0.

Sites like Facebook, LinkedIn, Twitter, You Tube, and so on are the top-visited sites. It is on the grounds that systems administration is quite possibly the most fundamental necessities in this day and age. Productive systems administration is sponsored by the web. Along these lines, 66% of the absolute number of web clients visit web-based media sites every day. It has become a dependence on many. Again this carries numerous benefits and inconveniences alongside it. Not many of them are:

4.2.1 BENEFITS

- Make an enormous and solid organization.
- Expansion in various companions.
- More communication prompts a higher trade of information.
- Fabricate solid connections.

4.2.2 DRAWBACKS

- Individuals are exceptionally subject to the web to organize.
- Wastage of time.
- A high number of fakes and programmers.
- Individuals these days are so dependent on refreshing their Facebook and LinkedIn accounts that they don't understand the measure of time they are spending on such exercises.

As indicated by a study, each individual working in an association invests a normal energy of around 40 minutes every day via web-based media sites. This brings about a misfortune to the associations as their important and learned workers are caught up with visiting on the web with their companions.

4.2.3 STEPS TO ELIMINATE WEB 2.0 ISSUES

- The associations are finding a way the accompanying ways to dispose of this issue.
- Associations these days block all online media sites.
- They urge workers to enjoy exercises coordinated inside the organization, where they can mingle and unwind.
- An intriguing workplace can assist representatives with focusing more on their work.

4.2.4 USE AND EFFECT OF WEB 2.0

- Adobe Flash, Microsoft Silverlight, and JavaScript are utilized as rich web innovations in conveying web 2.0 notwithstanding Ajax, RSS and Eclipse.

- Its applications depend on the revamped download philosophy that made BitTorrent so productive that each downloader of substance is likewise a worker, sharing the responsibility and making the substance more open.
- Likewise Read: Top 10 free site speed test devices to get execution bits of knowledge
- It very well may be an amazing bait for an undertaking; with intuitiveness promising to bring more workers into day by day contact at a lower cost. The utilization of web 2.0 innovations and apparatuses helps more noteworthy investment in activities and thought sharing, consequently preferably prompting better idea out plan and more proficient creation, fortifying securities with clients and improving correspondences with accomplice.

4.2.5 TECHNOLOGY INVOLVED IN WEB 2.0

- **AJAX**: An abbreviation got from "Offbeat JavaScript and XML." AJAX is a significant basic innovation used to make intuitive Web applications. Ajax is the thing that empowers Web 2.0 locales to act progressively, so they feel more like PC programs than static site pages. Like the manner in which Google Maps allows you to drag components across the page? That is AJAX in real life.
- **Molecule:** An organization for the partnership of online substance, iota capacities as a fresher option in contrast to RSS (portrayed beneath).
- **Blog**: Originally got from "weblog," a blog is a basic substance site made with cheap independently publishing devices. Web journals are the foundation of Web 2.0's majority rule soul.
- **Mashups**: Websites or applications that consolidate content from at least one sources. For instance, Cellreception.com joins Google Maps with a data set of 124,000 phone tower areas to assist clients with figuring out where versatile inclusion is solid — and where it isn't.
- **RSS:** Shorthand for "Genuine Simple Syndication," RSS is a convention that makes it simple for PC clients to get content from their number one suppliers at whatever point the substance is refreshed. Rather than making sure to visit a site to peruse a most loved section, watch a video, or tune in to a sound program, RSS allows a client to buy in to the substance so it's conveyed consequently. The progression of substance the client gets is called an "RSS channel."

- **Web-based media:** A conventional term used to depict Web-based apparatuses that saddle the force of coordinated effort and gathering association. This can take numerous structures, from the individual site pages of MySpace to the virtual universes of Second Life to the expert systems administration well known on LinkedIn.
- **Labels**: User-created catchphrases used to depict online substance. Labels make it simpler for the two people and web crawlers to discover important and related data.
- **Wikis**: A powerful Web archive that permits clients to add, change, or alter the substance showed on the page. The client made Wikipedia online reference book is the most renowned model.
- **XML**: A shortening for "Extensible Markup Language," XML is a programming code for online information that jam the construction and organizing of an advanced archive paying little mind to whatever application is utilized to understand it. XML is a significant empowering innovation for RSS channels (depicted previously).

What are Web 2.0 devices or tools?

Web 2.0 apparatuses can extensively be characterized as end-client applications that require dynamic collaboration, person to person communication, or client interfacing among individuals and data. They quite often have going with sites and related applications for keen gadgets. In a Web 2.0 climate clients choose how they need to utilize, collaborate with, and make data. This differentiations with prior Web 1.0 conditions where one essentially read static data on the Web (Morrison and Lowther, 2005).Also, clients can create and control content from numerous areas in a Web 2.0 climate. Clients can add pictures, recordings, or connections to other media content. Understudies have limitless freedoms to individualize the substance they insert in their items, and the usability of these instruments energizes understudy inventiveness. Dissimilar to customary pen and paper type reactions, understudies are not restricted by their own imaginative capacities, page-length, or word tally limits. Understudies will regularly go past the fundamental assumptions for a task on the grounds that these devices work with understudies' innovative cycles. Natural instances of Web 2.0 destinations and apparatuses incorporate wikis and online journals (PBworks and WordPress), person to person communication locales (Facebook and Twitter), picture and video facilitating destinations (Flicker and YouTube), and applications to produce Web content for training, business, and social purposes (Wikipedia, Weebly, and Instagram). It is significant for educators to recall that the sorcery isn't really in the actual apparatus; instructors should initially consider their destinations for the exercise just as the motivation behind the understudy reaction project. The correct instrument can assist understudies with orchestrating their learning, connect all the more profoundly with the substance of an exercise, and interface with different students in more significant manners than customary reaction tasks or tasks.

4.3 WEB 3.0

It alludes the development of web use and cooperation which incorporates adjusting the Web into a data set. In empowers the upgradation of back-finish of the web, after quite a while of spotlight toward the front (Web 2.0 has for the most part been about AJAX, labeling, and another front-end client experience advancement). Web 3.0 is a term which is utilized to portray numerous developments of web use and cooperation among a few ways. In this, information isn't claimed yet rather shared, where administrations show various perspectives for a similar web/a similar information.

The Semantic Web (3.0) vows to set up "the world's data" in more sensible route than Google can at any point achieve with their current motor pattern. This is especially obvious from the viewpoint of machine origination instead of human agreement. The Semantic Web requires the utilization of a revelatory ontological language like OWL to create area explicit ontologies that machines can use to reason about data and make new ends, not just match watchwords.

The following are 5 fundamental highlights that can assist us with characterizing Web 3.0:

Semantic Web

The succeeding development of the Web includes the Semantic Web. The semantic web improves web advances popular to make, share and associate substance through search and examination dependent on the ability to fathom the significance of words, as opposed to on catchphrases or numbers.

Computerized reasoning

Joining this ability with normal language preparing, in Web 3.0, PCs can recognize data like people to give quicker and more pertinent outcomes. They become more savvy to satisfy the prerequisites of clients.

3D Graphics

The three-dimensional plan is being utilized generally in sites and administrations in Web 3.0. Historical center aides, PC games, online business, geospatial settings, and so forth are generally models that utilization 3D designs.

Availability

With Web 3.0, data is more associated on account of semantic metadata. Therefore, the client experience develops to another degree of network that use all the accessible data.

Pervasiveness

Content is available by various applications, each gadget is associated with the web, the administrations can be utilized all over the place.

4.3.1 BENEFITS OF WEB 3.0 TOOLS

1. A more customized perusing experience

- As intrusive as those adverts may now and then feel, there is no questioning the accommodation in having the option to effortlessly navigate to an exceptional proposal for something you truly need or need and that you may have in any case missed.
- Web 3.0 gives an undeniably more customized perusing experience for us all. Sites can consequently alter themselves to best accommodate our gadget, area and any availability prerequisites we may have and web applications will get undeniably more sensitive to our use propensities.

2. Better pursuit

- As noted beforehand, the capacity to communicate in characteristic language with a web crawler is unimaginably amazing. The expectation to learn and adapt turns out to be practically non-existent, and the advantages reach out a long ways past the purchaser; organizations can progressively adopt a more regular strategy to the site improvement on their sites, as opposed to falling back on interesting watchword methodologies.

3. More extravagant application encounters

- It isn't simply sites that will profit by the diverse Web 3.0 – web applications will likewise begin to offer far more extravagant encounters for clients.

- Consider a planning administration like Google, which is presently ready to consolidate the nuts and bolts of area search with course direction, inn proposals and live traffic refreshes. This essentially was absurd in the Web 2.0 time.

4. Advantages of decentralized informal organizations

- No focal position that catches information and utilizations it.
- Engages clients by remunerating them with some type of resource.
- Enhances the Web 2.0 interpersonal organizations in pretty much every manner.
- Secures the protection of the clients. Clients choose what they need to share and when.
- Large partnerships and associations lose ability to impact enormous enterprises.
- Decentralized interpersonal organizations are an extraordinary thought and can change how we think, share, and impart. In any case, numerous specialists question its true execution and keep thinking about whether it will work or not. Until further notice, we can just sit back and watch what they hold and offer sooner rather than later.

5. Trade Services

- With regards to the trade administrations, centralization isn't at all powerful. The greatest disappointment that we can see is the point at which the trade Mt. Gox got hacked. The hack cost them $460 million worth of bitcoin in 2014. Its worth would be at any rate multiple times all the more at this point.
- Decentralized trades are gradually filling in prevalence as they give a consistent client exchange insight without agonizing over any hacks or straightforwardness. This likewise implies that there is no concentrated position and no irreconcilable situation from the proprietor's side. They for the most part utilize many decentralized account applications to smooth out their administrations. As we definitely realize that the Web 3.0 relies upon trust, it is about decentralized trade. We should show a portion of the couple of decentralized trade benefits out there.

4.3.2 DETRIMENTS OF WEB 3.0

Less advanced devices will not have the alternative to manage Web 3.0.

Web 1.0 destinations will give off an impression of being significantly more obsolete. It will in general be extraordinarily jumbled for newbies to understand. Innovation isn't inside and out ready for it yet. Simple to get client's Public/private data. Individuals will invest more energy riding the web. Security strategies are required.

4.3.3 COMPARE AND CONTRAST WEB 2.0 AND WEB 3.0

Web 2.0

It is the "writable" expression of the World Wide Web with intuitive information. Not at all like Web 1.0, Web 2.0 works with association between web clients and destinations, so it permits clients to interface all the more uninhibitedly with one another. Web 2.0 supports interest, joint effort, and data sharing. Instances of Web 2.0 applications are Youtube, Wiki, Flickr, Facebook, etc.

Web 3.0

It is the "executable" expression of Word Wide Web with dynamic applications, intuitive administrations, and "machine-to-machine" collaboration. Web 3.0 is a semantic web which alludes to what's to come. In Web 3.0, PCs can decipher data like people and cleverly produce and disseminate helpful substance custom fitted to the requirements of clients. One illustration of Web 3.0 is Tivo, an advanced video recorder. Its chronicle program can look through the web and read what it finds to you dependent on your inclinations.

4.4 CASE STUDY ABOUT WEB 2.0

4.4.1 Wikis

Wikis are a sort of Web 2.0 application that takes into consideration expanded cooperation and coordinated effort (Knobel and Lankshear, 2006). In contrast to a blog, a wiki client with legitimate access can adjust any or the entirety of the substance posted by another client on the wiki whenever. Moreover, wikis offers a substantially more powerful arrangement. Made by Ward Cunningham in 1994 and named after the van at the Honolulu Airport in Hawaii, wikis are a kind of web application that makes it simple for gatherings of individuals to cooperate in virtual conditions (Chawner and Lewis, 2004). A wiki can be characterized as an assortment of pages intended to empower any individual who approaches contribute or alter its substance utilizing an improved on markup language. As indicated by Treleaven and Cecez-Kecmanovic (2001), wikis can be utilized to help the learning interaction; to broaden the educational plan; to animate inspiration and confidence; to permit understudies to cooperate, accomplish common perspective, and co-make information; to permit understudies to finish errands outside of class; to help the improvement of long lasting learning abilities; and to gets ready understudies for what's to come. Wikis support shared exercises by giving a configuration to the accommodation of commitments, an approach to sort out and update the site, and programmed upkeep of the connections among pages and to outer sites without the need of understanding or creating refined Web-building abilities (Clyde, 2005).

Progressively, wiki applications are utilizing a What You See Is What You Get (WYSIWYG) innovation, which implies the interface looks and carries on a lot of like basic word handling applications, making it particularly simple to utilize (Fitch, 2007).

Higdon and Topaz (2009) investigated the utilization of wikis and online journals to help an instructing technique utilizing these Web 2.0 apparatuses to accumulate understudy reactions to inquiries on pre-class perusing tasks for college understudies in a mathematical examination course educated during two diverse eleven-week terms. Since the innovative necessities of Web-based encouraging techniques may keep a few teachers from viably executing such strategies, this article likewise investigated the mechanical prerequisites of wikis and online journals, and the substance explicit inquiries that keep a few educators from utilizing them. The creators utilized evaluations as a quantitative measure, and understudy reactions and perceptions as a subjective measure. In investigating the information, the creators tracked down that the utilization of wikis and sites in this setting assisted with encouraging profound, applied arrangement obviously material while additionally assisting with establishing learning conditions that line up with Bransford, et al's (2000) four anti-extremisms of constructivists learning conditions: student focused, information focused, evaluation focused, and local area focused. The creators additionally tracked down that the utilization of Web 2.0 advances like wikis could be utilized in a wide scope of orders, with minimal mechanical overhead and negligible educator responsibility suggestions. What's more, the creators accomplished the entirety of their expressed educational objectives, which included encouraging dominance objective direction among understudies by zeroing in on the basic abilities, standards, and systems expected to finish an undertaking or play out a capacity, which advances a local area focused climate; advancing meta-psychological reflection among understudies, which upholds an information focused climate; advancing the dynamic exchange obviously ideas, which additionally upholds an information focused climate; reacting to singular contrasts among students, a focal element of a student focused climate; and expanding the measure of effortful time that understudies go through working with the material, giving expanded freedoms to criticism and more opportunity to realize, which is key to a gainful appraisal focused climate.

Notwithstanding, the creators additionally tracked down that amount relies upon what teachers will do to cultivate this sort of learning. Accordingly, the creators recommend that future exploration ought to give more data about the level of achievement of such a methodology, and propose further acclimations to more readily meet the adapting needs of understudies.

Matthew, Felvegi, and Callaway (2009) investigated how adding to a class wiki influenced the learning of pre-administration instructors, the two students and graduates, selected three language expressions strategies classes more than two semesters with an emphasis on how adding to a class wiki influenced understudies' learning of the course content, what were understudies' view of adding to a class wiki, and what innovation concerns emerged when utilizing a wiki. Utilizing a contextual investigation approach, information assortment sources included online perceptions, understudy reflections when the movement, email correspondence, talk with records, and specialist notes. Subsequent to breaking down the information, the creators tracked down various advantages from utilizing a wiki. Concerning adding to a class wiki influenced understudy learning, the writers found that utilizing a wiki prompted a more profound comprehension of the course content, improved maintenance of the material, understudies expanding on one another's work, more cautious perusing of the course reading material, and support of homeroom exercises and broadened study hall conversations. What's more, the utilization of a wiki permitted understudies to make expanded associations between courses in their degree program, proficient improvement meetings, mentoring meetings, outside readings, and Internet research. As to's insights to adding to a class wiki, the creators found that understudies found wiki innovation actually valuable, understudies showed expanded responsibility for learning and endeavors, and understudies had substantial thoughts for future employments of wiki advances. At last, in regards to the specialized worries that emerged when utilizing a wiki, the creators found that while trend setting innovation abilities were not needed, a few understudies' innovation concerns uncovered that they needed innovation abilities. Thusly, the creators gave a few suggestions to improving the utilization of a homeroom wiki. These included appointing jobs, doling out various degrees of admittance to the wiki, and showing understudies how to appropriately post with references.

Hazari, North, and Moreland (2008) explored the instructive worth of Wiki innovation by recognizing its relationship with factors that may have the potential for improving student results. The members of this investigation were understudies in an undergrad college business course. The creators created and tried an overview to quantify mentalities towards learning and instructional method, inspiration, bunch association, and the utilization of innovation. These four speculations were tried to decide whether factors like age, sex, work insight, and web-advancement experience affected understudies' fulfillment with the utilization of wiki innovation. Subsequent to dissecting the information, the creators found that wikis can advance cooperation in bunch tasks, can empower arrangement, and can make understudies OK with this new age of innovation instruments. What's more, the creators found that by utilizing wikis understudies can fabricate altogether on one another's information by shaping participatory networks. Since the objective of wiki innovation is to advance understudy commitment, the creators additionally found that instructors should utilize participatory methodologies in which clients become dynamic supporters and makers of substance. While this investigation zeroed in on the utilization of wiki innovation in a business college, the creators accept that extra exploration is expected to investigate how Web 2.0 advances identify with understudy learning, perspectives, inspiration, and student results. The creators additionally suggest examining wikis in various educational plans and teaches.

While Web 2.0 advancements like web journals and wikis have been concentrated in different advanced education educational program zones and these investigations have recognized various huge advantages to instructing and learning, the utilization of such Web 2.0 innovations in legitimate training has not been as widely examined.

4.4.2 BLOGS

The term blog is short for web log. While sites are a kind of Web 2.0 innovation, online journals are commonly content-related. Blog entries will in general be composed by a particular gathering of individuals who give data and understanding, like specialized specialists, or individuals with extraordinary perspectives or composing styles. Individuals look through the posts on a blog in sequential request, in a design like that of perusing a journal or diary.

Churchill (2009) investigated the utilization websites with a class of post-graduate understudies in a data innovation program with an emphasis on finding the manners in which a blog climate can enhance study hall educating and lead to improved learning encounters. The analyst gathered information through perceptions, examination of blog exercises, relics, constant instructor reflection, interviews with chosen understudies, and a survey. The creator tracked down that the survey proposes that the understudies concurred that publishing content to a blog worked with and added to their learning, and because of the utilization of online journals, that the facilitator gave off an impression of being more engaged with their learning. Furthermore, the understudies concurred that the facilitator's contributing to a blog action urged them to blog. The writer likewise tracked down that the parts of publishing content to a blog that contributed most to the understudies' learning were getting to and perusing websites of others, both those of different understudies and the facilitator; accepting remarks; reviewing finished assignments of understudies; and perusing individual input. The meetings demonstrated that what understudies preferred most about writing for a blog was seeing crafted by others and accepting remarks on their work. At long last, the specialist found that appraisal was a significant factor in inspiring the understudies to take part in the contributing to a blog segment of the course. What's more, while understudies demonstrated their readiness to blog later on, whenever needed to do as such by a facilitator, they showed up less willing to keep publishing content to a blog all alone to help their learning without being needed to do as such. Nonetheless, in view of these discoveries, the creator recommends that online journals can be viable and valuable exercises for learning. Moreover, by using websites, an instructor can establish a climate that assists understudies with feeling that they are significant pieces of the study hall local area, and that their necessities and suppositions are perceived and tended to. At long last, to augment openings, these parts of a blog can be extended through other Web 2.0 applications, as wikis.

Yang (2009) inspected the utilization of online journals by English as a Foreign Language (EFL) understudy educators in two instructor preparing programs at two science and innovation organizations as an intelligent stage in their preparation measures. The exploration addresses controlling this examination included what kinds of reflection were engaged with understudy students' appearance, what were the instructor coaches' jobs during the time spent publishing content to a blog, and how could a blog advance basic reflection and a local area of training. The creator broke down the members' postings on the blog, overviews of the members' intelligent encounters utilizing the sites as reflection devices, and the members' gathering intelligent exchanges recorded by the teachers in class gatherings over the execution of websites during the course. The analyst found that understudy educators effectively examined showing hypotheses and their suggestions through websites. The entirety of the web journals of the members were intelligent, and some fundamentally considered their contemplations and offered critical remarks. What's more, the scientist found that educators would challenge understudy instructors' speculation by posting inquiries and posing for additional appearance to raise members' basic reflection. A lion's share of understudies announced that because of such difficulties by the teachers, their reasoning went further and turned out to be more basic. Moreover, the members thought about innovation as a valuable stage for reflecting and speaking with one another. At long last, the analysts found that writing for a blog accommodated more opportunity for the members to reflect and talk about course content, which lead to basic reflection. What's more, a local area of training is driven by the way toward venturing back, reflecting, and investigating. Besides, when utilizing online journals as a stage for reflection, the creators found that members were managed the cost of more freedoms to offer remarks and challenge each other's perspectives, and they could discuss or communicate thoughts that had been forgotten about in the conventional homeroom. This exploration study is relevant in that it distinguishes how a wiki could be organized and used to help cooperative learning, just as numerous positive understudy insights in regards to communications and coordinated effort utilizing Web 2.0 advances.

While sites have been effectively used in schooling and have been found to make critical, positive commitments to the learning interaction, sites have limits.

Above all else, the configuration is restricted; the postings on a blog show up as an online diary with new passages showing up in sequential request. Likewise, when a posting has been made, it must be altered by the first creator of the post, and frequently just inside a restricted measure of time. Clients of a blog can't adjust the postings of others on the blog; they can just offer remarks as a different post underneath another client's posting. Accordingly, while all commitments to the blog can be seen by all clients, the information and adjustment of substance on the blog is restricted to a solitary individual. Besides, the postings on a blog can get unimportant or obsolete after some time. Be that as it may, while wikis give similar benefits as a blog, wikis are substantially more powerful and enjoy various upper hands over websites.

4.5 CASE STUDY ABOUT WEB 3.0

4.5.1 LEARNING WITH 3D WIKIS

There is an enormous space for leading exploration identifying with the educational advantages of instructing and learning in 3D virtual universes. As of late a few electronic 3D virtual universe. Teachers may lead classes in a wide range of settings inside a 3D virtual existence where they can connect in genuine like climate of a class. Instructors and students may cooperatively lead meetings from topographically scattered areas in a common virtual 3D space. They can permit instructors and students in leading gatherings, classes, introductions, computerized presentations where students can come and connect like a similar way we do in our reality. 3D virtual universes accessible today and in coming future will be useful across a different scope of orders including instruction, medication, business, trade, science, correspondence, media, workmanship, engineering and plan, law, software engineering, language learning, history and topography to specify yet a couple.

4.5.2 INTELLIGENT SEARCH ENGINES

Over the most recent couple of years, taking in measures have profited by the innovative development of the web. The scattering of the web has allowed the presentation of new instructive cycles, which are more adaptable for getting to the assets for learning. Presently a days Internet has become the most helpful and incredible wellspring of data. To adequately manage the immense measure of data on the web, progressed web crawlers have been produced for the assignment of recovering helpful and important data in media structure for its clients .When you utilize a conventional web index, the motor can't actually comprehend your pursuit. It searches for Web pages that contain the catchphrases found in your pursuit terms. The web crawler can't tell if the Web page is really important for your pursuit. It can just tell that the watchword shows up on the Web page. A Web 3.0 period of Agents based-web search tool could discover the catchphrases in your inquiry, yet additionally decipher the setting of your solicitation. It would return important outcomes and propose other substance identified with your hunt terms. Specialists accept that Web 3.0 will furnish clients with more extravagant and more applicable encounters. Specialists additionally accept that with Web 3.0, each client will have an exceptional web profile dependent on that client's perusing history. Web 3.0 will utilize this profile to tailor the perusing experience to every person. That implies that if two unique students, each played out a web search with similar catchphrases utilizing a similar assistance, they would get various outcomes controlled by their individual profiles .Understudies will likewise profit by information development controlled by the Semantic Web. A Semantic Web Agent based web index will return a media report instead of simply a rundown of hits. A brilliant specialist can return neighbourhood addresses, applicable web journals, books and TV programs about the point to the student. Ontologies will interface the student's requirements and qualities so that customized specialists can look for learning material dependent on the students' necessities. Students can apply similar sort of search prospects with other media articles like picture, sound, and video. A few instances of this sort of innovation can be found on programming like Ojos Riya photograph sharing apparatus that permits to naturally label pictures utilizing face acknowledgment, or Like.com which empowers the client to look for items dependent on comparable pictures.

4.5.3 ONLINE 3-D VIRTUAL LABS/EDUCATIONAL LABS/SIMULATIONS OR 3D WEB

3D rich graphical UIs will go about as an amazing stage for the clients to take part and perform cooperative exercises, sharing outcomes and trading media data among members in a more characteristic manner. Coming up next are a portion of the instances of 3-D Virtual Labs/Educational labs/Simulations or 3D Web based applications that will shape future schooling:

1. To visit puts those are not open: Visiting better places in virtual universes would profit students from numerous points of view. Antiquated where understudies can reach there in a little range of time for all intents and purposes. For instance, to investigate antiquated spots like Tajmahel, Red stronghold or Rome, Students can connect and encounter with the climate of the spots, different understudies and can have their instructor as guide through the web. Also, they can see the Egyptian pyramids or visit an Egyptian town similarly. There is such a lot of degree where we can show the understudies and give them a protected and monetary method of encountering such things.

2. To advance understudy joint effort: Students can meet up and meet basically in different and appealing way. They can team up and work on normal tasks. Understudies and Educators may have conversations, talk, interface, and visit on the normal ventures. Also, they can fly over and move things around in a 3D world. They can even utilize and work in different 3D universes momentarily.

3. To advance appraisal through Project Based Learning: For example, understudies can do explore and make a (virtual) town in, say, the Roman Empire. Also, an entire gathering of understudies all throughout the planet could establish this climate while going to a distance

adapting course. This way they can cooperate on an undertaking and ready to encounter the fascinating methods of learning a ways off.

4. To foster situations and reproductions: High end designs and rich 3D web applications can be used to make reenactment based conditions or Labs where students can learn or even do tests. These Labs are supposed dry labs. These Web based Labs can end up being very helpful for online students. They could go to a vivid virtual science lab to do tests. After the recreation, understudies could go disconnected into a genuine science lab to play out the right test and perceive how it functions. Undeniable level logical trials could be led, and master specialized preparing could be gotten, in manners that a college or school couldn't bear. For instance, envision dividing molecules, leading a medical procedure, flying a plane or investigating cold conditions.

4.6 EXAMPLE CASE STUDY WEB 3.0

4.6.1 SIRI

Web 3.0 is pushing the web ahead to where utilizing the fingers to convey will turn into a relic of times gone by. All things being equal, applications like Siri that utilization voice acknowledgment programming are turning into the flood of things to come. Truth be told, voice acknowledgment programming is turning into the critical part of Web 3.0.

Siri is the ideal illustration of where Web 3.0 is taking PC clients where their machines will actually want to impart to one another and furnish clients with better list items. For instance, increasingly more Siri and other individual associates will actually want to offer convincing responses to questions asked by proprietors rather than the irritating "I don't have the foggiest idea."

For a very long time, Siri has been tolerating not very many orders that it can follow up on. This incorporates basic errands like updates and headings to the nearby supermarket. These have been cultivated by pre-customized calculations in the iPhone that can just do fundamental ventures of the web to concoct similarly essential answers dependent on store area. Also, this is if the store has a site that shows headings obviously in any case the query items can be deluding.

4.6.2 FACEBOOK

Nonetheless, with Web 3.0 asking Siri how to fabricate a woodshed would yield bit by bit guidelines without alluding.

Indeed, even as many are anticipated the end of Facebook in view of the progress from Web 2.0 to Web 3.0, this forecast is by all accounts deluding. All things considered, the long range informal communication part of this online media goliath will frame the base foundation for the manner in which the web is utilized. The organization has been welcoming individuals to make new social orders that will flourish with Web 3.0. This is their triumphant technique as these individuals who have been welcomed have wound up making 300,000 Facebook applications from tests and games to computerized endowments which have supported client commitment on the stage.

By giving the Facebook API to designers, the organization allows engineers to arrange their tests item audits, and games. Thus, Facebook has promised itself life span and another reign in Web 3.0.

4.6.3 WOLFRAM ALPHA

This is a computational insight stage where one can figure answers and it is particularly utilized by understudies and experts from various fields like math, sustenance and science among others. This stage utilizes Web 3.0 by get-together data for clients from data sets on the web and smoothing out the data for end clients.

On this stage, one can type in an inquiry and it will decipher the inquiry and yield results applicable to the setting of the inquiry. For instance, when one sorts in a nonexclusive proclamation like "two cups of strawberries", Wolfram Alpha will give you the healthy benefit, various calories and some other complete data relating to two cups of strawberries. For this situation, it gives you beginning stages for additional examination.

For explicit inquiries like "Where is Ecuador?", it will give an unmistakable response to the inquiry and afterward go on to give associated information that can assist the client with being capable instinctively and normally answer their inquiry completely.

REFERENCES:

1. http://computersight.com/software/cloud-computing-chapter-one-review-and-guide/. Accessed March 23, 2013.

2. http://2.bp.blogspot.com/. Accessed March 23, 2013.

3.http://cloudstrategypartners.blogspot.in/2013/04/intercloud-not-all-same-ederation.html.

4. http://www.cse.wustl.edu/~jain/cse574–10/ftp/cloud/index.html. Accessed February 24, 2014.

5. Poehlein, S., V. Saxena, G. T. Willis, J. Fedders, and M. Guttmann Moving to the media cloud. Available [Online]: http://h20195.www2.hp.com/V2/GetPDF.aspx/4AA2–1000ENW.pdf (accessed August 15, 2010).

6. The role of standards in CloudComputing interoperability. Available [Online]: https://resources.sei.cmu.edu/asset_files/TechnicalNote/2012_004_001_ 28143.pdf. Accessed February 24, 2014.

7. He, Y. The lifecycle process model for cloud governance, 2011.

8. Engelbrecht, A. P. Computational Intelligence: An Introduction, 2nd edn. Wiley Publications.

9. Garg, S. K. and R. Buyya Green cloud computing and environmental sustainability. In S. Murugesan and G. R. Gangadharan (eds.), Harnessing Green IT: Principles and Practices. 2012, pp. 315–340.

10. Kliazovich, D., P. Bouvry, and S. U. Khan GreenCloud: A packet-level simulator of energy-aware cloud computing data centers. The Journal of Supercomputing 62(3): 1263–1283, 2012.

11. Baikie, B. and L. Hosman Green cloud computing in developing regions Moving data and processing closer to the end user. Telecom World (ITU WT), 2011 Technical Symposium at ITU, Geneva, Switzerland, October 24–27, 2011, pp. 24–28.

MIX
Papier aus verantwortungsvollen Quellen
Paper from responsible sources
FSC® C105338

Printed by Books on Demand GmbH, Norderstedt / Germany